RIOTOUS LIVING

a book of cartoons
by

Rowel Friers

" *Calm yourselves. The
news to-night is terrible.*"

BELFAST

BLACKSTAFF PRESS LIMITED

1971

3rd Impression

© ROWEL FRIERS 1971

Published by
BLACKSTAFF PRESS LIMITED
84 Wandsworth Road,
Belfast BT4 3LW

SBN 85640 000 9

Printed in Northern Ireland by Belfast Litho Printers Limited.

Bud

INTRODUCTION

Politicians are not in good odour in Northern Ireland at the present ti
are blamed for landing us in chaos. They have been too moderate, too extr
compromising, too unyielding, They are approaching the state of lost credibil
began across the Atlantic with Lyndon B. Johnson and now creates gaps on b
of the House at Stormont. The citizens have stopped listening to their leaders

Well, they had better listen to somebody, bend an ear to some message
or that faraway light at the end of the tunnel will get no closer. One Ulster v
rather hand — that deserves attention is that of Rowel Friers, a consiste
campaigner for tolerance whose cartoons in this book have been collected u
apt, if frightening, title of "Riotous Living.'

It is not merely the function of funny men to amuse. They possess the
shock us, too: to use their gifts of irony and satire to bring us to our senses; to
us to have, in the Ulster phrase, "a titter of wit."

Friers has not shirked that responsibility. We see a sense of it developi
collection progresses. In the first section, with drawings from a period before
Ireland's nightmare began, his subjects have a cheerful inconsequentiality — ove
beaches, forgetful elephants, hirsute schoolboys, club bores, garden parties at
instead of demos, the greyhound owner whose dog thinks he's being bedd
when he is put in the trap.

Was that all we had to worry us in those days? Friers made us lau
dilemmas, trivial though they might be.

Yet he was always a political animal as well, alive to the absurdities of t
scene and viewing them with the sympathetic eye of one who, because he lik
has resisted invitations to spread his wings in London.

He shows us Lord Brookeborough saying to himself "This is my own,
per cent of my native land"; a King William for the day being reminded by hi
he feeds the chickens, that it is time for his Majesty to head the procession
O'Neill picking petals off daisies — "They love me, they love me not."

He notes the scheming and jockeying for position in the Unionist Party with a mordant eye — "The Unionist Party must be the only one in parliamentary history with a built-in opposition." His enthusiasm for O'Neill's successors in the Premiership is restrained. He shows us the men in control, with Orange, Republican and Civil Rights sashes around their necks, piled into a rickety Northern Ireland jalopy, backfiring its way along a rough road well posted with danger signs, Brian Faulkner at the wheel.

In the last section, the signs having failed to call a halt, horror and compassion take over from political satire. This is an Ulster with its Red Hand bleeding — many red hands now. A child holds his teddy bear with the Sword of Democles poised over him; another weeps in a street covered with missiles, while faceless and heedless men rush by, carrying clubs.

The book ends with a gunman sprawled in the gutter in a pool of blood. Sean O'Casey supplies the caption; "Take away this murderin' hate."

It now is the reaction of a civilised mind to the madness gripping Northern Ireland. Friers grew up in a household that blended the artistic with the humorous, and both good art and humour are incompatible with bigotry. His brother Ian, the sculptor, encouraged his drawing, which began at an early age, and got him a job as an apprentice designer and lithographer.

"I was born with a silver propelling pencil in my mouth," Friers says, and his bent remained towards the cartoon. His first work was published in Pro Tanto Quid, the Queen's University rag magazine, but the first drawings for which he was paid were accepted by the Portsmouth Evening News, the result of a contact which his brother made in the Navy.

For a while he played the role of a prophet without honour. He appeared in the pages of Blighty, London Opinion, Men Only, Punch and Reynolds News before he began a long association with Dublin Opinion. The three Dublin morning newspapers, the Times, the Independent and the Press, also used his work. Now he is a weekly institution in the Belfast Telegraph, and a frequent illustrator of local television programmes.

It is remarkable reversal of the familiar odyssey of the Ulster writer or artist, who first establishes himself in his own country and then feels the tug of the metropolis across the Irish Sea, where opportunities and rewards are greater. Friers was offered a staff job with the Daily Express in London at one stage, and had it not been for the intervening serious illness of Arthur Christiansen, the Express's dynamic editor and a man for whom he felt he would have liked to work, he might have taken it.

Why does he prefer now to stay in Northern Ireland? "I know the people here," he will tell you. "It's as simple as that." Yet his cartoons are not parochial — and the adjective could not be applied to the more serious vein which the latest turn of events has compelled him to explore. His early success in England laid the foundations for a style that is international in appeal, and his contributions to Dublin Opinion had to be geared to their syndication in other magazines in different parts of the world.

The greatest influence on his development has been American, rather than English, and he admires the New Yorker school. He does not hold in similar esteem the political cartoonists in the American Press, whose curiously old-fashioned approach is one of the paradoxes of the country which, in other fields, has established new frontiers of humour and wit.

In the final analysis Friers is his own man who has blended his influences in a highly individual style — urbane in outlook, skilled in drawing, painstaking in detail, and lively in its imaginative quality. He is sometimes accused of revealing an "anti-abstract" bias, but his antipathy is confined to the phonies of that school. Like the comedian who wants to play tragedy, he has done "straight" work in the visual arts as well. Northern Ireland would be a poorer place if he ever forsook his first love.

Ralph Bossence
1971

ACKNOWLEDGEMENTS

The cartoons in this book originally appeared in the following publications: the Belfast Telegraph, Dublin Opinion, Fortnight, and the Sunday Independent.

YESTERDAY

"I thought we'd never get the darned thing free from that scrum!"

Doc, I think I have a bad touch of the 'Flu!

" *Well, well, well, if it isn't old Pringleberry !* "

"*Don't try to rush me, Kate . . .*
don't try to rush me."

" Don't talk to me about the price of coal."

"He refused to go back to school unless they let him keep it on."

"Ach, and me doin' so well with me New Year resolution."

"Well, if New-a-Zealand can fiel' an ALL BLACK side – why not South Afrika?"

"It doesn't seem the same without old Casey!"

"I declare that child gets more like his father every day."

"Four prompts in one night and you call yourself and elephant."

"Dammit, I can't see anything obscene in the naked body, can you?"

13

"Moo-o-o-o !"

" We've been working to the wrong scale all the time."

"This is it . . . Gibbon's 'Decline' and ———"

"It's those dreadful Hassans. Pretend you don't see them."

"Of all the weeks in the year you have to pick Derby Week."

" . . . . and, at the risk of appearing a bore ——— "

"Go on – have a bite, Adam!"

"I suppose we should offer to help the P.M. with the washing up?"

LEST WE FORGET – AGAIN

Party Politics

"Here they come — darn it!"

"I hope we're not keeping you folk out of bed?"

"There's a Goldfish in my brandy!!"

"Pop says you've a higher cubic capacity than a stratocruiser, Mr. Flynn"

"And then there's the one about....."

"Another rhubarb wine, Mr. O'Flannigan?"

Lord Brookeborough Speaks

"Breathes there the man with soul so dead,
Who never to himself hath said,
'This is my own, my 18.75% of my native land ! . . .' "

Next you'll be trying to tell me there's no such person as Lord Brookeborough.

The Unionist who asked, "Just what was this Covenant?"

Golly ! – That doesn't look right

" . . . . cha, cha, cha "

" I could promise you all sorts of things,
but you are far too intelligent an electorate
to believe that election promises are ever
carried out."

"Time your Majesty was off
to head the procession !"

What the Cartoonist enjoyed most in 1966

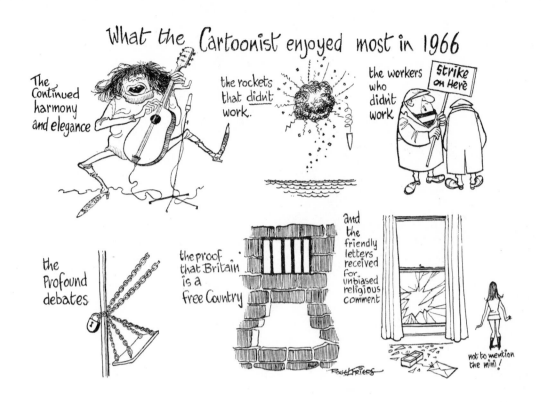

The Continued harmony and elegance

the rockets that didn't work.

the workers who didn't work

strike on here

the Profound debates

the proof that Britain is a Free Country

and the friendly letters received for unbiased religious comment

not to mention the mini!

THE OLD FIRM

HONEST Sean

HONEST Sean

"... but the hours are long and the pay could be better."

FILL 'EM UP,

"A happy and prosperous . . . aw forget it !"

*"Why did my mother ever put me into
the Civil Service ? "*

"Having passed sentence, may I now take the opportunity of wishing a Happy New Year!"

Kinetic Komment

I think it symbolises life – Just keeps on going until it finishes

Can I have one for Christmas

symbalic

S'diabalic

Fascinating

"It's strange, but all he can think of is mint sauce."

"First Wedgwood-Benn, then Alec Douglas-Home — and now Freddie Gilroy"

"This way, stupid!"

"Psst!"

"Forty love"

"Cut out this love stuff, Buster!"

" Prunella ! Prunella darling — He has just said 'Pater'! "

" – Paradoxically, we find in Picasso an equivalent amount of aestheticism as in, say, Leonardo or Peter Paul Rubens."

"If my pop did pictures like that I'd leave home."

"Gee fancy Aeneas leavin. that poor dame Dido
flat like that !"

"Which way for the Galway Oyster Festival ?

'Look we've just seen the first man !'

"They haven't left room for the choir – how about the congregation ?"

"He's got a new angle on bird imitations."

"Gosh ! Big folk ! !"

"Aw forget it — if we tell them they'll not believe us anyway."

"Doggone it ! I seem to be quicker on the draw than the artist !"

"Take some dictation, Miss Ryan."

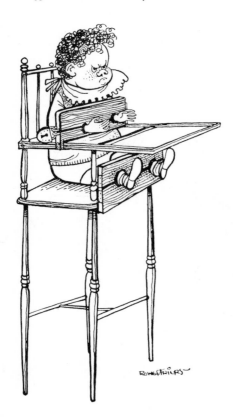

Do I detect a note of sarcasm when you say "is this bus goin' to the Transport museum?"

"I'm charging you with driving without due care !"

"I told you the turn of the stairs was tricky."

"Let me tell you guys, in the States at this time we have what we call St. Patrick's Day – an' boy, that sure is something!"

"Only a few steps from our back door' –
that's what it said !"

"The Laundry sent us the wrong parcel."

"I hope you have your woollies on, darling!"

"I hope we are not expected to dress for this confounded party !"

Edith ! Edith ! — We've only got a fortnight!"

"Like I say, come in September and have the place to yourself!"

"It's not a bit like the book."

"I wish i'd known about this toothpase sooner"

"No, two minutes from the sea at LOW TIDE !"

*"I put all my spare time into building it — then suddenly I lost
all desire for a yachting holiday."*

"It simply means whereas I walk with the old fourpenny, I trot with the new fivepenny."

TODAY

"I know it must sound dreadful — but I'm ashamed to be Irish."

"For you I'd like to see more resolutions and less revolutions."

"I started off with hopes. All I can do now is to wish you better luck."

"Goodwill to all and peace in the '70s."

"Personally, if I were the P.M. I wouldn't want them all behind me, I'd rather have them in front where I could watch them."

"The way I luck at it — watt diz it matter watt we think, no buddy pays no heed annywey."

"Fault ! fault ! fault ! What do you take me for — the Government"

"Successive governments have been making monkeys out of you for so long, I feel the time is now ripe for my party !"

"They say he feels strongly about it."

49

THE CARTOON by Rowel Friers published in Saturday's "Belfast Telegraph" showing the Cabinet rendering that now familiar street ballad "We Shall Overcome" was soon to bring a note of dismay in the Friers household.

Where was Herbert Kirk, the minister of Finance?

Rowel, who tells me that it was just a slip of the pen, offers his apologies to those readers who may have thought that a crisis within a crisis was in the offing and to Mr. Kirk who may have been refleeting on the qualities of his singing voice.

"I wuz just sayin', doesn't it seem awful quiet without them"

Rowel Friers looks at the Ombudsman-to-be

"Come now, one at a time, please!"

" . . . They love me, they love me not ... ?"

Rowel Friers backs O'Neill

"Christmas mail me fut ! – They're all for the P.M."

says: It's funny how one's M.P. during the election campaign has . . .

cunning of a fox . . . the ferocity of a tiger . . . the wisdom of an owl . . . the tenacity of a terrier . . . the strength of an elephant . . . but ends up just another back bench mouse.

"I think I'm half-a-crown short !"

"Green's an insult till Ulster — the breathaliser shud turn orange."

"I mind the days when you had to stand up for your rights."

"Sit-in? — if y'wud sit in the house more often ye'd make less of an eejit af yerself."

"What did you say this river was called?"

"We are bad enough on this Zcar theme without you giving it the Twist!!"

"Subversionary!"

Twelfth Parade

"Gosh, what a time to have a Splittin' headache"

"I painted it white so's me wife can pick me out on T.V."

"I think it's nice to see the students walking instead of thumbing lifts."

"Look at it this way fellas — we'll be setting an example to the grown-ups by respecting the ban."

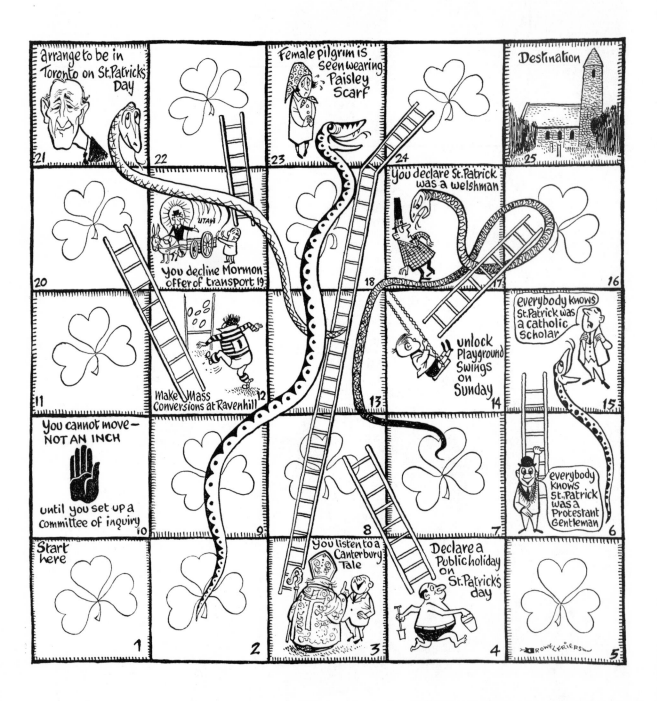

58

"Derry ? — Why you can't even see IRELAND !"

WE SHALL OVERCOME

Gentlemen, this is a battle at Scarva, not a garden party at Stormont.

"Let it not be said that I'd see the procession ruined just because the oul' white mare had colic, !"

"I see the U.S. lunarnauts are walking on the 21st."

"Its one thing being with it, Charlie, but is this not a wee bit too forward looking ?"

61

The trail of '69

"I haven't had a night's rest from thon barricade went up – me bed wuz
in it ?"

"I didn't know Capt. Long had gone and called in the NAVY !

"I didn't think I was coming back to clear up on the home front"

"I'd say the new Governor didn't expect the climate here to be as hot as the Bahamas."

"Civil disobedience's daft – how can y'be civil if y're bein' disobedient?"

Rub-a-dub-dub, five men on a tub

"Now we shouldn't have any trouble getting the broken flags to finish our crazy paving."

"The Unionist Party must be the only one in parliamentary history with a built-in opposition."

A HAPPY CHRISTMAS

NEW LOOK

TUES. WED
& THURS
SERMONS
by
THE
MINISTER

It's time we made our voice heard .

The new master

"And for the next trick I need help from the audience."

Cuckoo in the nest ?

"Some of the pupils don't realise that silence is not always golden."

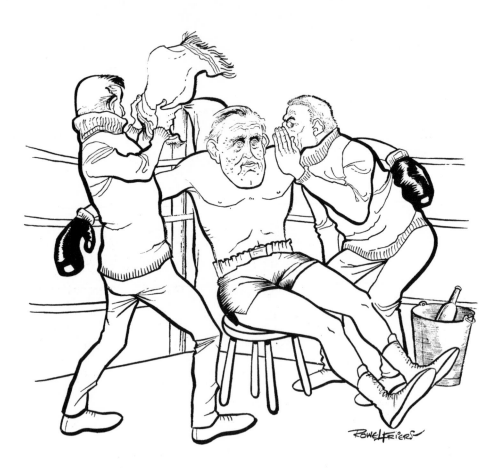

"Look out for that right swing"

'. . . . . and we don't worry about the currents — it's the undercurrents'

'And remember the word is charter-not hijack'

..... And the amazing part of the act is
that the rope is not tight nor is it held firm at
either end.

*Sure if you had till listen till thon craters in Stormont it wudn't only be yer ears – yer head wud
be bizzin'*

"We've got a wonderful country if we could control our climate."

'And they call us stupid'

"Which of you fellas is going to settle permanently in Northern Ireland ?"

"If I could only co-ordinate those wings I'd be flying"

"A word in your ear ... the solution to the problem is ...

"This one is serious – it's a threat from the Inland Revenue !"

"Grandpa says we're ascended from humans."

SHADOW OF A GUNMAN

"O.K. Boys, we've some tough jumps ahead."

Raoul Frere
Presents His new season's collection

Missile-proof two-piece for the late night reveller

Steel Duncher and Shatter-proof Visor for the Casual Knockabout

A NEW national costume

Two-tone reversible cloak ideal for the Party (Political, of course)

and for the latter-day "Stone age" man — in Black sheep's clothing

THE MEN IN CONTROL

"... NEWS TIME !"

84

"It should be a winner if we can get it to go."

THE RED HAND OF ULSTER

HAPPY NEW YEAR

Rowel Friers spells it out

"Now we've made it how will we control it?"

Design for a
Peace Memorial

Cloud over the Island

'Will the helicopter be replacing you ?'

Irresponsible act.

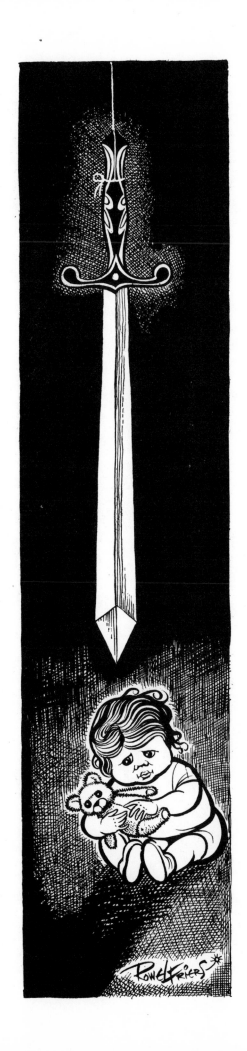

THE RED HANDS OF ULSTER, 1971

RETURN OF FRANKENSTEIN

"Take away this murderin' hate"